RUNNING for TRAP DOORS

Joanna Hoffman

Alexander, Arkansas
www.SiblingRivalryPress.com

Running for Trap Doors
Copyright © 2013 by Joanna Hoffman

Cover design by Sibling Rivalry Press.

Author photograph by Emily Rose Kahn-Sheahan.

Cover photograph by Stefanos Papachristou. Used by permission.

All rights reserved. No part of this book may be reproduced or republished without written consent from the publisher, except by reviewers who may quote brief excerpts in connection with a review in a newspaper, magazine, or electronic publication; nor may any part of this book be reproduced, stored in a retrieval system, or transmitted in any form, or by any means be recorded without written consent of the publisher.

Sibling Rivalry Press, LLC
13913 Magnolia Glen Drive
Alexander, AR 72002

www.siblingrivalrypress.com
info@siblingrivalrypress.com

ISBN: 978-1-937420-47-5

Library of Congress Control Number: 2013940168

First Sibling Rivalry Press Edition, August 2013

For my parents, Beth, David, Zoey, and for me.

Running for

11	Fences
12	Godface
14	Mile-high faith
16	Bloodbath
18	Golden
19	1989, age seven
21	High school electives
22	Why I had to leave the party early
23	Adding it up
24	Brooklyn primer
26	Sunday morning
27	Rush hour mob
29	Touch
31	My dad goes to meetings for parents and friends of lesbians and gays
32	Marathon training
34	Dear Sarah
37	Drunk girl
38	Surrender
39	Hangover
41	On claiming bathroom graffiti as my oracle
42	What I've been scared to tell you
44	The gift
45	Emoticon-English dictionary
46	Because I want you and I think you want me too, but we live far apart and you're really bad at text messages

Trap Doors

47	Folding minutes under the table
48	Pundit
49	Snap
50	Facing it
52	On child pornographer Eric Toth's naming as Osama Bin Laden's replacement on the FBI's Most Wanted List
54	What 19-year-old me should have said to the girls who rolled their eyes when I handed them cards for the rape crisis hotline
56	Skeleton
59	During the ninth plague, Miriam reflects
62	Clean love
63	After
64	Sick day
66	The mole people
67	A living will for my niece, in reverse chronological order
69	Drawing blood
70	On learning to open my eyes
71	Pride
74	Welcome home
75	Everything I have been waiting for
76	The I of the tiger
78	Grand Canyon
80	Trap door

RUNNING for
TRAP DOORS

Fences

This ribbon is something
I knew by name once—
a smooth, greaseless
sling of bone cradling
what seeps unguarded.

To learn *protection*,
what it means when
applied to myself,
when I am so used to
stitching my own swelter,

calling the fever home
with the mouth of the match,
the spark means *lighthouse*,
the burn speaks *lullaby*,
the coo of cracked skin

will not know me now.
This is what *therapy* and
remedy forget—that I love
the sound of my own
heart breaking,

the delicious crash
stomping the embers
back to frenzy. It's calm
that terrifies me: silent
snowstorms in the night,

how they blanket, in a fine
proud skeleton, the shivering
earth, its novocaine twitch,
100 songs with their mouths

taped shut.

Godface

On the days when Grandma picked me up from
elementary school, I tried to run to the car before
she leapt out in her purple sweat suit and pearls,
pink lipstick crayoned onto her teeth, screaming,
Godface! Over here! Come over here so I can rip your face off!

There was no use in asking Grandma not to call
me Godface, or yell out about mutilating me to
the entire class. She was officially Too Old to
Give a Fuck, using her fake ID of Crazy to laugh
at funerals, sing her order to waitresses, channel
the fervor of serial killers into love for me.

The winter I turned sixteen, Aunt Marcia's cancer
grew malignant. I sat in the hospice lobby with my
Chemistry books. Next to me, Grandma reapplied
her pink lipstick for the third time that hour.
The smell bathed my throat in melting plastic.

My father held my mother's hand as she sobbed.
I put my book down and watched them.
Grandma poked my side, hard. *Don't you dare cry.*
Her voice a sharp, hot wire.

Instead, I started talking to her about the Law
of Conservation of Energy. I told her that after
this, I no longer believed in God, but in
everlasting energy.

She didn't respond, just stared at her purse.
Are you listening? I asked.
Yes, yes, I just think that's stupid.

After Marcia's funeral, my parents dropped
Grandma and me off at her apartment.
She shouldn't be alone, my Mom whispered.

Grandma walked straight to the kitchen,
pulled on an apron, and told me to sit
at the table. I stared all around me at the
portraits on the wall: my grandfather's baby
blue tie at their wedding, my grandmother's
siblings squirming in a family photo in the 1940s,
my mom and aunt as little girls on their first
day of school. Somewhere in my chest, there
was a maelstrom of black water, churning.

Plate after plate appeared before me: brisket,
green bean casserole, noodle pudding. I gaped
at them, as if they were someone else's birthday
presents I accidentally unwrapped. I swallowed
it all—the sweltering grief of that tiny apartment,
the guilt I didn't really understand.

When the first wave of nausea ripped
through me, I dropped the fork.
Grandma, I'm sorry, I just can't.

I looked up to see her, standing in the
doorway, holding a plate of potatoes.
For the first time in my entire life,
I saw a tear slide down her cheek.

What do you mean?
You're not even trying.

Mile-high faith

On the airplane, I find Jesus.
My Jewish mother would be horrified,
but she isn't here, on this hamster-sized
plane thrashing like a baby's fist through
the question-mark sky.

If she was, I imagine she'd scream.
Instead, I am praying. Head skyward,
clenching the armrest as if it were
the hand of the last beautiful moment
I want to stay alive for.

If someday is now, Jesus, I'm sorry.
For every stupid, stupid moment
I held an empty bottle like a doorknob
I was waiting to turn and just listened
to the bell of last call booming
over me, a rusted rocket.

The man next to me, the one with no
understanding of personal space or
inoffensive cologne, smiles at me.
It's just turbulence, he says, patting my leg.
I'd like to use his arm as a ripcord.

Jesus, please. No one on this plane
loves me. There are no beautiful girls
whose necks I could use as sedatives,
no men who frown like my father.
It's not fair, Jesus. If I knew for sure
we were crashing, I probably wouldn't
call anyone, anyway, because what is
there to say that I haven't said?

*I believe in Jesus. Just thought you
should know that about me.*

Well, I don't. I hate to admit
I believe in dumb luck and in
lazy statistics. Chances are,
everything will be fine.
Most likely, you can write
any poem you want to
on a day that works better
for your schedule.

Sure, you can love me
whenever's good for you,
whenever you decide
you believe enough
in the impossible,
the invisible,
the name
you never thought
you'd call out.

Bloodbath

> *In 2011, the UK Department of Health lifted its ban on gay men donating blood, as long as they haven't had sex with another man in the past year.*

Say there is a clean song
jackknifing the fat from
bone. The bleach runneth
over from your good, fine
hands. Father, I have sinned
because I would not fake the
flush, the fractured breath
like a dusty wafer on
your meaty tongue.

Say I am unholy because
I backed away from your
spray-on purity. I forgot
how dark you keep
your bedroom. That you
gagged the doorbell,
held the phone at gunpoint,
threw darts at her shadow
to keep it from twitching.

Is my blood a dead ocean?
Is there something political
in the man who squeezes
my hip on the subway,
or in the way I thrust a pen
into his palm? Is my body
too choked to serve? Should
I not teach your children to
raise blades from their wrists?

I'm telling you, I have my own
army now. We found our own
holy in the murder of shame.

We have suitcases of blood
to set sail in the ocean.
If you won't take them,
we are burying them
where they were born—
a baptism by salt.

Golden

My mother told us
we had to fast on Yom Kippur
to cleanse our sins,
then ate a package of saltines
right in front of us.

I'm sick, she snapped. *It doesn't count.*

—

When you pulled my hips
to yours in the server station,
whispering,
Don't tell anyone, okay?
I felt my neck flush the hue
of a swimming pool filled
with braided chains, marinating rust.

Your ring digging into my side
was the smallest voice,
whispering, *You're a girl. It doesn't count.*

1989, AGE SEVEN

My father asks me
where I'd like to eat lunch.

This is an honor. I kick my feet
in excitement. Say, *Chinese!*

There are no kid's meals
at Chinese restaurants.
Just heaping plates
of greasy chicken and broccoli.
My father eats nothing. He says
he isn't hungry.
When I start to slow down,
my father stares at me—
his eyes: cups of black tea.

You wanted to eat here. So finish your food.

I keep going until I feel
like I might vomit.
When I finally push the food away,
he throws down cash
and tells me it's time to go.

When we get home, my mom asks us
how lunch was.

I didn't eat anything. Joanna wanted Chinese.

He makes a tuna sandwich and puts on
the television. I lay on the floor,
pretending to read a book about
butterflies. I am really watching him,

trying to understand.
The light from the TV flickers
all afternoon. His face
does not change.

High school electives

Shop class is for boys and lesbians. Not starfish like you that sit faceless and unscreaming as they slice your limbs. *It's okay,* you say, *I can grow more.* You love the smell of thirsty metal, of a grind that drowns you in the belly of its noise, the snowdrift of splinters and how a steady hand can birth something new. You think they can't see you under the mask and smock, the bulky gloves. You are still the girl with torn cuticles and the face of someone used to eating lunch in the bathroom.

Home Ec is in the brightest room. The oven timers are *tsking* at how slowly your breasts punctuate the run-on sentence you've become. Your roast is all wrong. The blood washes over the gummy flesh and you wonder if you are the last girl in your class who hasn't yet had her period. Maybe you really are a boy. Who would marry you with your knobby knees, with your sour cupcakes and bland soup? No wonder you grew up with a taste for boiled eggs and sardines from the can. No wonder your recipe book is full of Chinese take-out menus.

Creative Writing is the last class of the day. Afterwards, half the kids stay to work on the literary magazine. All of the submissions are anonymous. When yours fills the screen, you bite the inside of your cheek. *Let's talk about the narrator,* Ms. Nowak says. More than anything, you want to think of her reading your poems. *Look how the writer speaks about their desire for a woman. What does that tell you?* Someone yells out, *it's written by a guy.* Ms. Nowak nods. Yvonne, who hates everything, says, *I like him. I vote yes.*

Why I had to leave the party early

I don't fit in here. These girls can smell the TV dinner
on me, the metro card
and the borrowed shoes. These girls smile
like checks ripped from the book.

How the gleam makes everything
come unhinged. Even their eyebrows
have bling. Even their issues sparkle.

Yesterday, we flew to Paris for lunch.

*Occupy Wall Street is probably the only occupation
these people will ever have.*

I have Target breath. I bought my fingers
at McDonalds. I sold my sex drive
for pot. I sold my cocaine
for laundry detergent.

You're a poet? Do you get health insurance?

Last night, I ate a bowl
of late fees. They tasted
like home.

Adding it up

Trust is one part forgetting and three parts
blind hope. Knowing there has never been
a ladder you didn't slip from, but look, you're
already climbing.

Sleep is three parts trust and four parts letting go.
The release is a clenched wire coaxed to feather,
an exit sign clearing its throat to welcome you in.

Morning sex is seven parts trust, seven parts awe
at what was no dream. When she bends forward
and rests her forehead against yours, the dawn
washes you in.

Wanting is five parts pull, three parts still.
Standing by the shore and watching the riptides
tangle and unravel, breathless, at your toes.
You forgot this could be easy.

Hope is all you have made from this.
Hope is all that is left. The reason
you never settled. The door you
forgot you had left open, but look,
you're already through.

Brooklyn Primer

After Dean Young

Avoid repetitive acronyms.
ATM, not ATM machine.
Don't even think your PIN number
is yours alone, ever.
The barrel of unique thoughts
bottomed out long ago, and so
forgive yourself for passing up
the chance to write a script
about Abe Lincoln as a vampire.
Now be your own muse.
Give your fear a pen name
and then get drunk and forget it.
If you're sad, sigh loudly at the DMV.
That's not a spiral you're in, it's a leaky
faucet you've been orbiting for years.
Your electric bill might be the love letter
I've been waiting for my whole life.
My metro card may be your pink slip.
That's not a flu shot, it's a hangover.
That's not your 401k, but if the Messiah
is coming then it doesn't matter.
Nothing is for sure, but we've seen
it all before.
You wanted certainty and expected what?
A hammock? A trust fund? A room full of noise?
You enter and exit the world alone, but so
does everyone else.
The most comforting words I ever heard
I found in the crease of my grandmother's brow
as she lay in the hospice bed.

I had just told her
not to be scared, and she looked at me
as if it were the most absurd thing anyone
could have said.

Sunday morning

Up the block,
there is a burly, tattooed man on his stoop
cradling something in his hands.

Closer now, I see it's a baby macaw
shaking and clucking softly,
too small to know its beak
could crack the bones of the fingers
stroking him gently.

My dead bolt shatters.
I want to tell him,
*You are the last person I ever thought
I would see caressing a baby macaw.*

His son watches from the window,
eyes wide as the bird's.

Come here, he yells to his son.
I want to show you something.

Rush hour mob

After Les Murray

All me pour into the yawning metal mouth
of the Brooklyn-bound D train. The shrill
hawk shriek of the gears is a dinner bell
we all lean to, sighing soldiers.

All me swing eyes to the one empty seat.
Green dress and swollen belly me
slides in, while the rest of me
balance on the back of the whale,
waving cell phones as if to conduct
gravity.

All me sway, undulating flock,
a chorus of downturned glances.
Untouchable me enters the train car.

Excuse me ladies and gentleman.
I am homeless and have two
small children. Please help.

The smell of urine bends the air
around me. Me backs away.
Me shuffles forward. The gray
in me strangles the prism.
Teenage dreadlocked me
pulls out crumpled dollar bill.
Ghost me says,
Bless you. There is a low shame
tugging at the seams of our shirts.
One of us almost wants to cry
but doesn't.

The train bursts into open air like

the secrets whiskey-lathered me
ladled out onto tablecloth
the night before.

All me stare at my phone. The vibration
means someone not-me cares. All me
spill onto the pavement and splatter
home. All me heat up the leftovers,
feed the cat.

All me lay in bed, chanting the mantra
of your kiss until I fall asleep,
the tangled constellation of me,
my spine, my very
own star.

Touch

I just saw two girls walking out
of the subway and could tell
they were about to hold hands.

As they walked, one pulled the other
closer by the waist, tracing her pinky
against the other girl's thumb.

I swallowed hard, looking around me
for a smirk or scowl, but no one
seemed to notice or care but me.

It has been so long since
I have liked someone enough
to untangle the barbed wire
from my palms.

I have held women I love by the arm,
cradled my head against their shoulders
and wondered if we looked like sisters.

Even the public kiss could be a *drunk thing*.
But this undeniable X-ray into the honesty
of movement makes the cells where my
shame whittles its fangs flash and flash,
a siren of cold sweat.

With you,
it was harder not
to hold your hand
than to hold it.

Across the room, I would watch
your knuckles, a bony surf of pulse,
and remember how you unwrapped
fever inside me the night before,
left white paint thrown over
the face of my fear.

When our fingers bowed into
each other and you smiled at me
like that, I had no language
for politics, just the
clean whistle of *yes*
in my ears.

No one else in this city
smells like you, smothers
my brain so the only
voice coming through
whispers *touch.*

My dad goes to meetings for parents and friends of lesbians and gays

When the facilitator asks them to share,
he tells the group,
I think it's a choice. But it doesn't matter. I love my daughter.

The other parents sputter and spit
hot oil. He sits, arms crossed,
and closes his eyes.

On the drive home,
he says nothing. The sky
fades from postcard blue
to greyscape
threatening to collapse
in splintering curtains.

When it does, it is not
any less beautiful,
any less sky.

Marathon Training

This is how to extend every breath
into soft staircase. You are scaling
a wall of undulating lung, tethered
to the shivering rind of spine
splayed open as a carcass of road.
Your pulse is a map in Morse code.

Before you ever learned the code
of escape routes—jamming breath,
as a rusted key, into stubborn road—
all you knew was movement. Scaling
the itchy rash of *wait* from your spine,
your surgeon feet sliced you untethered.

In high school, you learned to tether
your pace to the other girls, coding
your want to kiss her glazed spine
into the handcuff of your breath
to her face as you passed by, scales
flapping as red flags of open-mouth road.

You never won a trophy, but the road
tasted like ribbons. Every bare tether
an undressing of virgins, a blunt scale
of everything you drenched with code.
It felt like a tidal wave to unfold breath,
without apology, down coast of spine.

Even when you finished last, spine
bowing to feet, to throbbing road,
you had a furious army of breath
streaming from your lips. Untethered
from your coach's frown, her code
for *loser*, you beamed bright scales.

Through the years, you learned to scale
down heartache into shivers of spine.
They say it's chemical, how the code
of *sad* is translated by tongues of road
into *exhale,* how the sinew can tether
you back to the whitewashed first breath.

Now, you are shoving handfuls of stupid hope into bursting
spine. The road measures your pounding on a scale of one to
everything. You are not tethered to even yourself. *Marathon* is
code for *look what you've done, with your very own breath.*

Dear Sarah

This is your official notice that I will be
setting up my Gmail account to automatically
respond with this poem every time you email
me—spitting stupid small talk into my inbox.

So to answer the questions you weren't
really asking: *I'm fine, my mom is fine* and
yeah, New York is great.
And the one question you were asking
but didn't: *Yes.*

Yes, it has been two years since I was
just a bad waitress who loved you, and
you were a puppeteer who couldn't stand
the idea of loving a waitress. *You deserve
someone who will motivate you to get a real job,*
you told me as we stood in the hallway
of your new apartment, paint burning
my lungs and boxes ripped open
like flayed skin.

When I said that I still loved you,
you asked me why I would love
someone who didn't love me back—
as if this was something I should
have known by the way you smoothed
your hair down with shaking fingers
when I walked in.

Yes. Your nervous smile at my parents' house
on Passover; how you held my hand in the
gardens in Santa Fe and said we would retire

there; and the way your naked body spilt into
mine like milk onto a kitchen floor—I sold
all those postcards to Girls Gone Wild.

Yes. The first night I laid in bed with
someone who wasn't you, my plastic
skin melted and all these shimmering
organs lay bare, flimsy and floundering
like fish flashing technicolor deaths.
How dare you drag that dead sigh from
my stomach with copper wire. But still—
the only reason I let her keep touching me
is because she was there and you weren't.

Yes. I moved to the city you never thought
I would. Got a real job and an apartment
in Brooklyn. The girl who once ran face-first
into a cement wall painted like air doesn't
exist anymore. Now, I race the sun to the
Statue of Liberty every morning. Write
myself letters in beer bottles and mail them
home, and

yes: This is the first day I've thought about
you in many. On most, you are the amen
that drips like drool; the eyelash fluttering
eclipses to black out the dust; the kind of
reflex that could only have been taught.

And then you email. The subject line says
Hey with 7 exclamation points—each one
a bullet shot into a disembodied deer head
mounted on a wall.

When I told you I still cared about the girl
who broke my heart the year before we met,
you told me I was desperate.

Maybe I'm just not as scared as you are
to admit this. I've peeled this skin down
to citrus, and I know I can never write
you back anymore. But that doesn't mean
I don't remember the time you told me that
when I clap, it looks like I'm catching fireflies.

Don't you think I still have ashes on my palm
from touching you?

Don't you think they burn every time I touch
the subway handrail, even when I forget
why?

DRUNK GIRL

After Angel Nafis and Jon Sands; after Terrance Hayes

Drunk girl swimming through copper
Drunk girl a sizzling mosquito, has you on mosaic radar
Drunk girl winces from the sharkskin scrape of brittle air
when you pull away
Drunk girl hears her name echo through every wind tunnel
of bone
Drunk girl trains her mind on the thin scream of needle,
of *okay*, of *doesn't matter*
Drunk girl drunk-dialed her mom by mistake . . . whoops
Drunk girl falafel at 4am
Drunk girl would love to fuck up a cell phone, a Facebook page
Drunk girl is real sorry about the text she's about to send you
Drunk girl says, *all you ever wanted from me is the fuck you
licked from your fingers*
Drunk girl knows she never expected anyone to want anything
more than that
Drunk girl is an overflowing bowl of radon,
here hold this a second
Drunk girl parachutes from one circus to the next
Drunk girl anything to keep floating
Drunk girl has electric memories of a dead lover and nowhere to
plug them in
Drunk girl teeth black with bile
Drunk girl shake a robotic hummingbird
Drunk girl is real good at drowning out anything you say she
doesn't want to hear
Drunk girl tourniquet of exit signs to slow the blood
Drunk girl brain honeycombed into airport,
ripping the goodbye from your throat
like a power cord
before you can even
remember her name.

Surrender

Once, I kneeled in an alleyway and clung to shrubs
until they fainted in my hands. My throat was an
escalator of snake venom; a vodka curtain snapping
its wet fingers against the asphalt sky. The tornado
in my gut motoring on, and on, and on.

Inside the bar, the girls shrieked and licked salt from
their palms. I couldn't grab hold of the wheel of their
laughter. I wore a dress of pennies. I thought of pictures
in the zoo of dead seals with their guts slit open, coins
spilling everywhere.

I grabbed the phone and slung my voice onto the wire.
My friend came running through the ceiling. *Why would
you do this?* she asked. *I'm sorry*, I told her. *I'm sorry. I'm
sorry.* I shivered on her floor all night as the wires
unsnapped, one by one.

This was my second brush with death in three years.
I never told my parents about this one. After the first,
I called them from the ER to tell them about the
scorpion, the blood on my shoes and the $2,000
helicopter ride to the hospital.

As I held the phone, I could feel the shrivel in my
mother's voice. How her hands couldn't untie this
knot in me, or even call it by name. All she could
do is say, *please take care of yourself*, and hang the white
flag of her sigh from the highest tree in the yard.

Hangover

Claw through this hangover.
Find the email shining in
the disco cage of your skull
since its crash landing
the night before.
The vodka crowed,
respond right now!
but thankfully, the water
told you to chill.

You carved
a bed for this apology
in the back of your neck.
Two months late,
it crawls in,
closes its eyes.

It's all good,
you tell the pockmarked ceiling,
the bottle of ibuprofen,
yourself. Seven states over,
the girl who wrote you
presses her face
into the neck of
a woman who loves her.

I'm happy for you

isn't quite the truth.
You staple
the postcard of her face
over your eyes
when you come.

The vodka opens
its lipsticked mouth.
You press delete
before it can speak.

On Claiming Bathroom Graffiti as My Oracle

Black marker, I believe in the steady hand
of your wielder, trust in the calm, sober lettering.
I can feel the slow can crush of you in my chest
when you ask, *Who will love me now?* God,
I know that feeling. Tonight, a whiskey-throated girl
sang a cover of "Moon Dance" at karaoke,
and I forgot then that I decided two years ago
to hate that song, to hate any rummaging hand
into the shot-glass memory of us slow dancing
in her kitchen; in the moment I stuffed a rag
down the throat of my fear and kicked it
under the refrigerator.

I pull out a pen and write,
I will. Thrown back in the bag,
the pen and marker
clang together like a metronome,
a single thread of Morse code
spooling around my skull,
a lasso of noise
singing me home.

What I've been scared to tell you

Love, there are nights I've set wake-up calls
knowing I'd sleep through them in the morning.
I've welcomed ants into the floorboards with
trails of honey; coughed up the fever and wiped
my forehead with it. I've mapped out my own
escape routes and poured in barrels of concrete.
Mailed my rent check to every apartment I ever
lived in, except this one.

I've brought myself to the floor, clenching
my stomach with the hope this pain could
leave my body. Drunk-dialed my depression
and asked it to stay the night, the weekend,
the winter. Pinned the slow arc of her head
turning from mine to the door as proof
of how easily she walked out of it.

Love, I have those days. Love, I've shaken
hands with my fear and never even seen
my anger standing in the corner. I loved
picking at my scars til they bled and then
bandaging them gently. The pain and the
gauze felt like different breeds of cloud.

Love, I wake up from these days and begin
digging my way out. Wear cotton and blow
the tea before raising to my lips. Spend the
subway ride to work scrawling answers into
the crossword puzzle; treat myself to coffee
for preventing early Alzheimer's. Let the soft
voice raise up from the tide's underbelly and
say, *You are worth this. You are worthy of love.*

Love, I have spoken to myself and answered,
out loud, in public. I've said *yes* so many times,
it sometimes sounds like an alarm clock buried
in the ocean; sometimes feels like holding a
check I'll mail myself years from now; sometimes
tastes like honey when all my tongue ever expected
was poison.

The Gift

You were blanket, that's it.
I never listened to anything
you said that didn't make me smile.

That night, in the Ethiopian restaurant
on Charles Street, you wore a grey sweater
and told me you had left her, finally.
We had been dating for four months.
I thought you would be happy.

Once, you gave me a toy bird made out of twine
and actual feathers. I imagined this
was what serial killers gave each other
as Valentines. I decided to perch him
on my martini glass, then drown him.
I thought you would like it, you said.

I do. I love it.

But not in the way you thought.

Emoticon-English Dictionary

:)
    I like you.
    I like bread.
    I'm drunk.
    I just swallowed a goldfish.
    I just mailed a Chinese take-out menu to myself.

:(
    I'm sad.
    My goldfish died.
    You won't make out with me.
    My cat killed a cockroach and left it in my bed.
    I am so hungover, I just walked into the subway and watched three trains go by.

;)
    I want to make out with you.
    I want to borrow money from you.
    My keypad is stuck.
    I'm a motherfuckin' pirate.
    I just ate a hot wing and it splattered into my eye.

:/
    I just swallowed a staircase.
    I'm unsure of things.
    She still hasn't called.
    I just saw an infomercial featuring leopard unitards.
    Nelly muzak is playing in this elevator.

    I have no personality.
    I mean what I say.
    I'm Amish.
    I don't care if you're starved for two-dimensional depictions of emotions.
    If anything I've said here is unclear, then maybe you should fucking call me.

Because I want you and I think you want me too but we live far apart and you're really bad at text messages

When the phone vibrates and your name appears, I imagine the technology as a shoebox diorama. Back to back in the cardboard room, your finger presses send, and I flail for the phone as if it were the shoulder of a child running into traffic. When I read your message, followed by the wink-face emoticon, I grin stupidly, gazing admiringly at this little black rectangle. The emoticon is your mannequin, a shivering mirage of a proxy. I want to sit down, Barbara Walters-style, and ask, *When you said wink-face, did you also mean smile-face? What about kiss-face?* I am almost 30, and the most exciting part of my morning is receiving a wink-face text from a girl across the country. How about this: meet me in the land where emoticons go to die. It could be a coffee shop in Philly. When I tell you I want to know what's happening here, you say, *Well, I don't know.* We watch each other in silence, your eyes raking up my cheek. I untuck the breath from underneath your tongue. It awakens and scatters towards me. The waitress asks if we're ready to order, and I say, *No*. I reach under the table and hold your hand, as if it were a letter I wrote with mine.

Folding Minutes Under the Table

The hot water has been boiling
since 6:30.
Steam from the pursed metal lip
knits into gnarled, wet ropes braiding
in and around the silent kitchen.

Fever in, fever out.
A skinny green worm in the eye-socket
of the microwave pops and locks
to 6:37. 6:38. 6:39.
The kettle's whine drips
a net of bee stings across the cracked ceiling.

You still haven't called.
I've been waiting all night.
The phone is a plastic Nazi.
Somehow, that little vibrating fucker
has all the power over me.
I imagine that if I were to lift up
that tiny rectangle of battery,
a small fist would punch me right in the eye.

What was I thinking, really?
You knew you loved me
when you asked me how I would kill myself
and I told you,
I would fold myself onto the train tracks.
You bit your lip and leaned forward.
I stood perfectly still, re-scripting the scene
like I always do,
like you had asked me, *Will you be there when I get home?*
And I answered, *Where else would I be?*

Pundit

In the supply closet, you shoved me against
the plastic forks.
The crack of tines, dead fences levitated
by one-fingered hurricane—
this is how you beckoned
the tide of crickets
in my spine
to sing iceberg-gasp
loose around your neck.

His voice slithered out, cold.
You stepped back,
your eyes dripping
across the floor.
He entered the room smirking
and folded his arms.

This is where you've both been? Get back to work.

Later, he would talk to me
about politics.
Bleeding heart.
You think you're gonna save everyone?
You need to learn when to give,
to take.

Last week, I heard
he was fucking you
every night
in the swivel chair
in his office.
I imagine his lazy grin,
the easy sweat on his face.
How he thinks he finally bested me
after all these years.

Snap

The hardest part is not apologizing.
Is it better to be genuine or to be sorry?

I am rarely both, but always the latter. On the subway, the word rattles in my groggy skull like a neon maraca. It just falls out so effortlessly. On the phone at work, my voice wavers, limboing under a thin, invisible line. Customer service is all about smoothing down the exploding insecurity of people who need therapy and reassuring them that they're right, they're good, they will be rewarded for being obnoxious. *I'm sorry, here's your entitlement back.* Over text, with the girl who broke up with me and then accused me of being a bad friend—*I'm so sorry. I'll be a better jellyfish in the future.* Every time the cell phone shakes, I wince. I walk home furious. *Leave me the fuck alone*, I snarl at the cat curling around my foot. She stares back, wide-eyed, then yawns and saunters away.

Facing it

Inside my irrational fear
is a wind tunnel of backyards:
grass so thick and tall
we can't see our feet as we run.

I round the corner and don't notice
until it is too late.

The wolf spider,
casually draped into my path,
is a sticky disease
I was destined
to fall into.

Its hairy legs
crush into my face.
I smell metal pans crashing
to the floor.
My fear is the sharpest needle
in my throat, a syringe
of dislocated sound.

When I scramble to my feet,
my sister is behind me,
stunned.

I'm sorry for pushing you,
she tells me.

I shove past her
and keep walking.
I can feel a herd
of baby spiders

hatching from
every strand of hair.

My mom
will not believe me,
but I can feel them.

They are everywhere.

On child pornographer Eric Toth's naming as Osama Bin Laden's replacement on the FBI's Most Wanted List

This is a dream. You are a boy wading through smoke, smiling. Rolling your tongue across this dry bath; this crick in an old man's spine from bending teeth to toes in memory.

When your father and brother went down in plane crashes, you saw the power lines ripple and thrash, screeching snakes lunging forward.

Saw your mother's eyes roll backwards, the flame a thirsty anthem scripting onto her flesh with fingers of ash.

Your six wives and twenty-six children, strewn like Coke lids on the grey beach, on the cemetery that drools and drools, that names every patch of empty land a grave.

You wake up screaming.

You wake up screaming.

Your twenty-six children, the wives you made of them, strewn like grains of sand on a beach. Your skin is the best passport; an everyday renewal.

When she found out, your mother's eyes rolled backwards, the tide a soft eulogy, a shroud that drowns in mercy.

When your father and brother heard, they thought of your model airplanes. How you howled when anyone else touched them.

You wanted everything to be born a museum. To bind
and gag all that comes after. Your own growing body
was the last disaster. You follow the yellow smoke
to a boy, smiling.

This is a dream.

What 19-year-old me should have said to the girls who rolled their eyes when I handed them cards for the rape crisis hotline

Let this name rattle in your throat
like a rusted song you once knew
all the words to before you trained
your tongue to either sneer or stay.

When I woke up
to find my best guy friend's hand
slithering down my pants, I had
no words. He liked it that way.
Thought my silence was some
kind of metaphor he never
would have gotten anyway,
so why think about it? Why
dissect the frog you can't
bring yourself to look at
with the lights on?

It was years after I spoke it
that I offered it to myself.
It was fun to be the hero,
but something else entirely
to be on the other side
of the hotline, phone
mashed up against my cheek,
my mouth trembling as I lay
my voice on the ground,
waiting for the stampede.

Why is it called a hotline?
I think of wire snapping
in flame, of an invisible
electric fence. At the shock,

we both jump back, staring
at our charred fingers.

When I say *I will take care of you,*
what I mean is, *there's a first time
for everything.* I won't be my own
hero or monster, but I will be here,
now, from now on, my eyes open,
my heart a doorbell I can't stop
answering, *yes, I'm home, I'm sorry
I pretended not to be for so long,
the lights are on now.* If I've learned
anything about self-care, it's that
the word *selfish* is meant to disable
all the alarms. Don't let it. There
is nothing selfish about this.

Skeleton

I am a skeleton made of reeds—
all shivers of noise set acoustic.
I'm whispering symphonies,
prayers to the gods of vibration.

Remember that time you wanted to kiss me?
When you tore the ghost of swollen heart
through the window? It felt like skin quaking,
bones bending in humble prayer around
this hot throb made public, unconcealable.

I wanted to pluck that moment
from the air like a slick whiskey-kissed
ice cube from the bottom of the glass
seized with chopstick precision.

I always thought we would make out
one day because I already have your
taste in my mouth.

You tug the heat from my throat,
a lighthouse pulling in ships as you sleep.
You glow so hard, I wish I could
lean in to the caged sun under your skin.

You are white noise remixed into
the backbend of every shadow,
and I have my ear pressed to the
thin wall of dream, mailing you
Braille postcards in my sleep of
the shivers you ripple through me
with every glance.

I wish I could have been the one
to cut the cord of your fever,
to make your chest unfurl
like red paint in water
for the first time in your life.

But maybe what I was meant
to learn here is that I can't always
be the hero. So why do I break
for broken girls? 3am hanging
over my shoulder to dry as I
stumble through the swamp
of drunk Brooklyn.

You shadow bulimic,
coughing up the night and
wiping your mouth
on the satin horizon of your sleeve.

Your hair reminds me of Sunday—
I could sleep right through it.
I am an acrobat on the tightrope
of your attention
and I'm thinking about the backbend
of your thumb.

Your hands flex—
the knuckles flash white lightning
and I pocket the static,
thinking of what those hands could do,
how once your fingers folded in on mine
like Muslims bowing to Mecca.

If prayers can be origamied into prophecies,
then *fuck me if I'm wrong,*
but I think you want to love me.

My eyes are hotel maids
dusting out the silence.
I am so stagnant.
I am the air that hovers,
and you are the shadows—
a cannibal glutton,
a greyscale goddess,
a fence I can never scale.

During the ninth plague, Miriam reflects

Moses, this darkness is no shadow.

When you were told to stretch your hand upwards
and watched the world disappear, I know your blood
must have glowed then. What power there is in
choking the sun from the sky. The night is a mask
that fits everyone. What if I sat in our father's chair;
if I cast a baby girl down the Nile? How long would
it take the smooth-skinned Pharaoh's daughter to
realize the child in her arms would only grow to
scrub chamber pots or lay quietly for men who
will never know her name?

When it began, Brother, I knew this had to be
the act of a man. I watched the Nile swell the
stain of banished women made to sleep in the
Red Tent while their men shuddered as if blood
didn't run through their own veins. Only a man
would see this as malice—the thick song
whispering lullabies to the reeds as it crawled past,
on its knees, cooing to the fish as they flailed.

When the frogs came, he said, *Let my people go
so that they may worship me*. Here, come into this
brighter cell. Here, see what can be done with
the miracle of swollen pride. I caught a small
one underneath my bed. Felt its tiny pulse
thundering inside paper skin; a small hammer
pounding by an invisible hand.

The lice. The flies. A great tongue rooting
between trembling legs. The *no* made him

roar. Made the sweat snap in waves across
his grinning face.

Next, the goats fell to their knees. Aaron said,
at least ours will be fine. They all huddled at the
edge of the fence, ears bent towards the bleating.

Brother, you threw soot skywards and watched
their skin erupt into craters. It's easier now,
when they no longer look like men.

You brought the hail, then the thunder and
firebolts *that I might show them my power.* Men
huddled under their wooden tables, clutching
the napes of their oldest sons.

How long will you refuse to humble yourself before me?
Come, locusts. The world is a softer place
without you. The insects crackle their wings and
the sun shudders, blinks, slinks like a doe-eyed
drunk under the horizon.

Here we are. You raised your hands and it was so.
Darkness that can be felt. All the Hebrew homes still
shine, the flames in our lamps thrashing gleefully.
Pharaoh can't go much longer, Mother says. She feels
blessed that her sons have their ears pressed to the
chest of God, that she was the vessel that made this so.

Moses, this is the closest you will ever come
to understanding. Outside, the night is a hunger
swallowing its own tongue. All the prostrations
in the world will never be enough.

You are starting to wonder how this will end.
You are careful now to speak softly when
he's in the room.

You are starting to feel the dark.

Clean love

*On the discovery of a possible marriage
between Jesus and Mary Magdalene*

Holy. Holy parchment. Holy body and blood of Christ. Holy revelation. Holy house of God. Holy house of a God and his wife. Holy marriage bed. Holy Pope brow furrowed. Holy woman, disciple among disciples. Holy eye to eye at first light. Holy cleanliness. Holy heart bent towards the pitch of her laugh. Holy laughter in the dark. Holy midnight wrapped like shroud. Holy undocumented anniversary. Holy breakfast in bed. Holy first kiss. Holy heartbeat watching the first nail hit flesh. Holy first night without him. Holy wail gagged and buried. Holy woman, all this time. Holy what goes on behind closed doors. Holy stays behind closed doors. Holy clean love. Holy immaculate rewrite. Holy feminine as divine. Holy feminine erased. Holy woman's breath suffocated by holy hand.

Holy history. His holy story.

After

In the morning,
she drove you home
in silence.
Halfway to your house,
the tire blew,
the car rattling to a jagged stop.
Fuck. Fuck.
She punched the horn, over and over,
and then screamed, her voice a damp cloth
straitjacketing you
back to yourself.
You flung open the door
and started walking
before she could tell you
to get out.

Sick day

This is not a good day for me to save you.
My nose is running and my phone is dead.
The armies of ninja spiders rappelling
down my throat are not in love with you,
only with parachutes born of sneeze.

I get it—you've seen talkative drunks
on the subway stumble towards me
as if my ears were clean tablecloths
and they've been looking for
somewhere to splatter.

I am good at *runway*.
I've been speaking it my whole life,
ironing the itch in my pulse to
steady red lines, a welcome mat
you can see from the sky.

I know that when you looked at me,
you noted every emergency exit—
every escape chute of shut-eye swoon
into the quiet basement you store
your heroes in until you're ready.

And now, you are. Your tongue is a
suitcase unsnapping against my teeth.
And now, my prayer is: *Let my spine
be a ladder between me
and what I stand for.*

I am calling on the God of
not always this. I am not
what either of us remembered.
The next time we meet,
we will both be on the ground.

The mole people

You wore my stitches in your teeth. *The bling of broken things always tastes like an easy win.* Waterfalled a step ladder of the fairy tales you wrote me into. Told me, *I know that's when you became this way.* Held up her death; that swollen summer when I learned to pray again, when I ran around the Prospect Park lake for hours on end as if I could shotgun my breath from here to her hospital bed in Florida. Told me, *this is why you've been alone since then and why you always will be.* As if there was a *why* to all of this. As if you were there the moment I woke at 5am after whispering for hours *and then she opened her eyes* (as if saying something could give it flesh). I realized then she was there, in the room, and this meant it was over. As if you could run your fingers over my poems and feel the encyclopedia of me. Shake your head slow at the tragic mess of me. *Please keep your ambulances to yourself.* There is an equator between pity and understanding. Between spite and pity. Between skeletons and lines I never wanted to draw.

There is a promise I hold underneath my tongue. It's from a story I never told you; a poem I never wrote until now. The last night I saw her, we rode the subway home from her show. If she was angry, she didn't say it. If I was sorry, I didn't either. Three stops from my apartment, she stared out the window and told me, *there are mole people that live down here. They have their own society, and hardly anyone ever sees them.* The train seized to a halt. We sat there, silent. Neither of us looked towards the window. *If you look for them, you won't find them*, she said, leaning forward and touching my hand. I watched her fingers land on my palm. I said, *I know.*

A LIVING WILL FOR MY NIECE,
IN REVERSE CHRONOLOGICAL ORDER

For you, Zoey, this exhale that hits like a plane's softest landing, this mouth full of red parachute. The river of names haloed around the sick bed. *Mom, it's me.* Fever that never quite breaks, but washes you with the warm tongue of something wild's mother. Sleep is a kindness that pulls you taut on the thinnest line.

For you. A garden that smells like your grandfather's hands. Tomatoes, tulips and one scraggly crabapple tree that should not have survived the tire swings, the makeshift forts, the hurricane, the thick beard of snow. The quiet ferocity marrying roots to dust.

For you. The body as house. The apple-tiled kitchen you've waited your whole life to come home to again. A round wooden table that is clean but never tidy. A television no one speaks to. A bedroom whose darkness your heart clutches for every time you close your eyes.

For you. The clock pivoting its neck to show you its face. A hand on your wrist that you didn't expect to comb the glass into mosaic. The moment the sirens lay their flutes in the sea. When the door opens. When she pulls you inside.

For you. The nights with a phone pressed to your chin til dawn. Realizing that loneliness is a myth we keep relearning. That your most horrible secret is tamed the moment she shakes it out like morning laundry. The fear spills out, a glass overturned by a merciful wrist flick, by someone who knew you were never that thirsty.

For you. Your grandmother's laugh. Your aunt's thin smile. How you wonder what it means to look like somebody. How you don't remember what came before, but the cherry popsicle in your mouth has melted and ahead of you is a blacktop streaked with July sunlight.

Drawing blood

The waiting room is a snow globe full of starfish. Are we all floating? Is everyone still breathing? Check your pulses. Fill out your paperwork. Who was the last person who sucked the salt from your neck? When did you last inhale? Have you used a needle? Have you ever had an abortion? Why is your family in the ground? How will your cells turn against you? Cancer? Heart disease? Have you ever wanted to die?

The *no* rolls out, an obedient dog. She says, *good*. She hasn't looked me in the eye yet. I just want to know that I'm all right. I know one day, this visit won't go so well. The cancer is planning my surprise party, spinning cream streamers from milky white blood cells. *I hate this place*, the nurse tells me. The needle sings its thin voice into my arm. The chorus of red booms into vial, after vial, after vial. *That's all me*, I want to tell her. I stand and stumble forward. *Steady now*, she grabs my arm. *You got a ways to go.*

On Learning to Open My Eyes

The brightest sky is a blindfold stitched
with black rain. I think of the dog pacing
by the back door. *Control* clocks the moan
sprinting past the flinch, how I once trained
myself to tiptoe; to gag the *yes* tapping underneath
the ice; to vault the rip-roar tripping from
my tongue—a parade of magician's scarves
I want to keep pulling, pulling.

I am a master of Escape. Show me a body,
I'll show you an escape route. Follow the thrash
to Oz, to 1998, to a woman too ghost
to ever raise the alarms.

The first time I opened my eyes, I thought
of surfacing from chlorine. O, the sting
and the entire hive swarming into the
swimming pool outline of me. I look into
her eyes when the honey begins to drip
from her lips. She swallows my windows
whole. There is nowhere left to go but inside.

Pride

The summer I turned 15, my grandmother got me
totally smashed at a wedding in New Jersey.
Somewhere between the third ABBA song
and the fourth glass of champagne, she told me,
*You know, someday you'll have a wedding just like this.
And when you do, please don't let them play any disco.*

I didn't know how to tell her that I probably
wouldn't be having any wedding at all. That I
wore these bones like a voiceover when really,
I was in love with my best friend Kathleen.
I thought just maybe, if I held this itch
underwater long enough, it would float up blue.

I tried to claw the dripping want from my voice
whenever Kathleen asked me what I thought of
her boyfriend, snuffing out my drive-in imagination
and burning every lamp in my throat watching her.

I learned what shame feels like. I coated my skin
with postcard gleam, as if the best I could ever
hope for was to reflect someone else's shine;
as if some parts of me were better off drowned
in a swimming pool of white-out.

But it is not in our nature to cower
before the mirror like this.

A person born blind will tilt their head back
and extend their arms when they feel proud.

It is in our blood not to bake shame into our
bones, but to live boldly. And so now, all these

years later, here is my pride—

for every time I refused to allow the wet
blanket stare of strangers on the subway
smother this burn to hold her hand;

for every time someone told me, *Wow,
you don't look gay*, and I didn't say, *Thank you*;

for not letting my heart be strip-searched
by those who want to know if my love is
pure enough;

because I have committed hate crimes against
myself for years and I already know all of
the tricks.

So when my friend asks me why there is no
Straight Pride Parade, I tell her, *You can't
be proud of something you've never had to fight for.*

This is for every wedding I watched from
the sidelines; every fairy tale with stipulations;
every *it's a choice, it's a phase, you're disgusting;*
every swollen choke of shame I learned to
coat my throat with; every gay kid who
believed nothing would ever make this better
because *home* meant *break the parts of you that
don't fit into the plaster of who you're supposed to be.*

We already are exactly who
we are supposed to be.

Just last month, I woke up living in a city
where I could actually get married one day.

I think back to that wedding in New Jersey
all those years ago—

how I was the last one to leave the dance floor,
makeup smeared and beaming; how my
grandmother grabbed my hand and said,
I'm proud of you, with no *if onlys* or *buts*
clinging to the underside of her voice;

how finally, after all these years,
I am able to say the same
to myself.

Welcome home

This girl is just a girl. Not sleeping pill, not happy pill. Not bourbon Band-Aid.

The whole time we are at the bar, she sits close. Rests her hand on my leg. I think this means *yes*. But outside the train, when I thank her for inviting me, she says, *Oh yeah, sure. We're neighbors, so . . .* and pats me on the shoulder.

The whine of the G train slithers into my stomach. There is a waterfall of house keys down my mailbox throat for every stranger whose momentary affection made me dream of locks turning.

I am swept under the rug of my own house. Never allowed to hang posters on the wall. Suitcases still unpacked in the closet. I take off my shoes and tiptoe through the kitchen, as if I were a 15-year-old terrified of my parents waking and crashing down the stairs to smell wine coolers on my breath.

The lesbian bar is a post office where I constantly file for a change of address—always with the same crazed impatience, always forgetting I already have a home I never let myself live in.

Everything I Have Been Waiting For

The sunken clocks in my chest are graveyard alarms,
the panic button of *right now* trigger-locked to my finger.
My friend says, *I've never met someone so good at waiting*.
Where is my ribbon, tourniquet of hourglass sand?

The panic button of *right now* trigger-locked to my finger,
I'm looking for a girl who is her own beekeeper.
Where is my ribbon, tourniquet of hourglass sand?
I searched for her in shipwrecks, only found splinters.

I'm looking for a girl who is her own beekeeper,
heart slick with valentines written to itself.
I searched for her in shipwrecks, only found splinters.
This stale wanting, a rotten canyon growing moss in my bones.

Heart slick with valentines written to itself,
my magic 8 ball said, *Ask me again when you're sober*.
This stale wanting, a rotten canyon growing moss in my bones.
Realized this map I drew for myself is an impossible labyrinth.

My magic 8 ball said, *Ask me again when you're sober*.
I never really knew what it meant before.
Realized this map I drew for myself is an impossible labyrinth;
the fear of loneliness—a persistent gnaw on my heel.

I never really knew what it meant before.
Today I swaddled the itch, fed it breakfast.
The fears of loneliness a persistent gnaw on my heel—
finally stared them in the eye and watched them sink to the floor.

Today I swaddled the itch, fed it breakfast.
Nothing is wrong when nothing is wrong.
Finally stared them in the eye and watched them sink to the floor,
the sunken clocks in my heart, the graveyard alarms.

The I of the Tiger

It's not about you. The subway gate
is not an iron jaw refusing.
Even the girls who scratched
their skin translucent
as shower curtain liners,
made themselves ghosts or
dead butterflies pinned to loose leaf,
are not thinking of you now,
and were not then.

You, you dug shallow graves
the shape of beautiful girls
into your bed, and laid awake
night after night, timing your
exhales to theirs.
Your sadness was fear
with a pen name.

The first moment
her scowling mouth
dripped your name
from her lips like rotten meat,
you scoured the *I* from
every whistling wire
of nervous system,
tethered the grammar
of your world
into second person:

Are you okay?
Are you mad?
Do you love me?

I thought I looked familiar.
In the parade of ghost girls
flushing the color
from my face, I am
the very first one.

This is not about *you*
and neither am I.

Grand Canyon

> *"You say I am wilderness. I am."*
> –Toni Morrison

On my third morning hiking in the Grand
Canyon, the rocks began to breathe. The heat
sank low into the cupped palms of that serrated
dragon of dust. My favorite ghost stepped out
of copper stone, smiling wanly as if she wasn't
surprised to meet me here.

I probably should have turned back then, at
the first sign of my delirium, or when Sarah
slid down the mountain, saved only by a small
tree on a crumbling ledge,

or when the boulder fell onto my hand,
my nails blackening instantly and my
fingers closing in, trembling,

or even when we shook the last of the water
from our daypacks.

Realized we were fucked in a way West Baltimore
hadn't prepared us for—our throats, angry mothers
holding our tongues over flame for not thinking
this through.

That night, lying beneath the ceiling of tar
while a dead girl smoothed down my hair
and told me not to worry, I was not surprised
when the scorpion stung me.

I already felt myself becoming canyon.

Ten hours later, the rescue helicopter arrived,
a paper plane soaked in gasoline. *Look around you,*
the EMT said. *This ride will cost you two thousand dollars.*
I stared through him. Somewhere around us,
I could hear a voice combing through the static.
I wanted so badly to believe in this.

Like the canyon, I am shaped by what I miss.
Some nights, I still cling fast to the bruised
outline of her shadow. Still refuse to erase
her number from my phone, still roll over
onto her laugh.

Still wake up curled around the ghost of her
shape next to me, like a rusted scrape of earth
holding its dusty arms tight around the memory
of river.

Trap door

In another life, I was a programmer, or an engineer.
I love wires—flickering bones of a homemade God—
and how thy will be done or you buy a new battery or
you Frankenstein a scavenged perfection. Here, I can
teach my blood new tricks. Curve my tongue into a
conch to sound out words I have no shape for. Claw
safety into the bathroom mirror. Train my spine to
straighten every time I wince. *Yes, I love you*, and this
is something I hope I'm not dozing through. I keep
waiting for the wire to scratch the air, a record needle
that sings even when its throat has been cut. When the
bells ring, will I remember how I used to pray to my own
loneliness? All the hymns of waking in a quiet house
boom through the headphones. I taught myself that
wanting only bends us further into ourselves, turns
us into commas not trusting ourselves to ever declare
anything finite, a dictionary written in soft pencil,
last night you told me you loved me and I said, *thanks,*
not because I don't love you, but because I'm a rat
in a maze I keep forgetting I built myself and you
are the trap door I didn't see coming.

Acknowledgments

"Fences" first appeared in *decomP*. "Trap door," "On learning to open my eyes," and "Surrender" first appeared in *PANK*. "Pride" first appeared in *Sinister Wisdom*. "Snap" and "On child pornographer Eric Toth's naming as Osama Bin Laden's replacement on the FBI's Most Wanted List" first appeared in *The Legendary*. "Dear Sarah" first appeared in *Spindle*. Gratitude to the editors.

Gratitude

Thank you to Sibling Rivalry Press for believing in me and welcoming me with open arms. Thank you to my third grade teacher, Mrs. May, who told me I'd be a writer someday. Thank you Kate Nowak, my high school Creative Writing teacher, who told me to never stop writing. Thank you to my Baltimore and New York poetry slam families and my poetry family around the world. Special thanks to my amazing, brilliant friends who lent me their time, edits, love, hot sauce, kind words, and unending support—Chris August, Jeanann Verlee, Caroline Rothstein, Megan Falley, Jared Singer, Sonya Renee Taylor, Omar Holmon, Victoria McCoy, Liz Bowen, Gayle Danley, Twain Dooley, Alex Zimmerman, Karen Garrabrant, Jessica Stuart, Angelique Palmer, Andrea Gibson, Karen Finneyfrock, Rachel McKibbens, and other people I'm probably going to kick myself for forgetting. Thank you to my family for being great and loving me. Thank you to Amanda. Thank you to Katie for being my life coach for the past sixteen years. Thank you universe, for making my dream come true.

About the Poet

Joanna Hoffman is a poet, teaching artist, and LGBTQ advocate. Her poems have appeared in *PANK*, *decomP*, and *Sinister Wisdom*, and in *Milk and Honey: A Celebration of Jewish Lesbian Poetry.* Joanna facilitates poetry workshops for LGBTQ youth and has featured at venues around the world. She lives in Brooklyn.

About the Press

Founded in 2010, Sibling Rivalry Press is an independent publishing house based in Alexander, Arkansas. Our mission is to publish work that disturbs and enraptures. We are proud to be the home to *Assaracus*, the world's only print journal of gay male poetry. Our titles have been honored by the American Library Association through inclusion on its annual "Over the Rainbow" list of recommended LGBT reading and by *Library Journal,* who named *Assaracus* as a best new magazine of 2011. While we champion our LGBTIQ authors and artists, we are an inclusive publishing house and welcome all authors, artists, and readers regardless of sexual orientation or identity.

www.ingramcontent.com/pod-product-compliance
Lightning Source LLC
LaVergne TN
LVHW041345080426
835512LV00006B/610